Ray & Jani Ortlund

YOUR FAMILY IS GOD'S PLAN

His Mercy from *Generation* to *Generation*

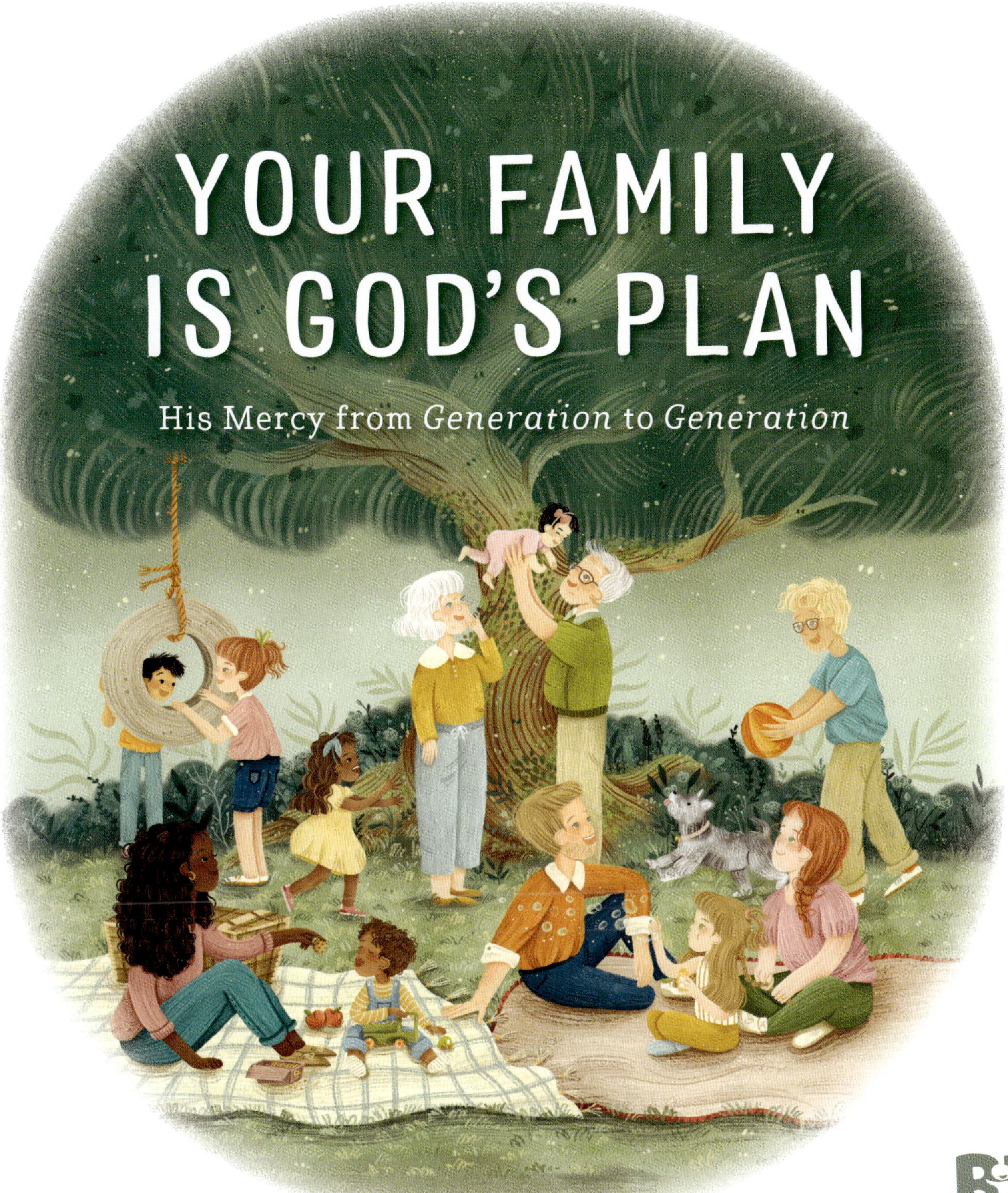

B&H Kids
Brentwood TN

To our great-grandchildren yet unborn—
may you set your hope in God.
Psalm 78:7

Published by B&H Publishing Group, Brentwood, Tennessee

978-1-4300-8853-0

Dewey Decimal Classification: C306.85
Subject Heading: FAMILY \ PROVIDENCE AND
GOVERNMENT OF GOD \ FAMILY LIFE
Printed in Shenzhen, China, March 2024
1 2 3 4 5 6 · 28 27 26 25 24

What is your family like?

Is it big and loud? Small and quiet? Your special family is unlike any other family on earth!

Think about how many other families you know. You probably can think of a lot—the family next door, the family you play with at your favorite park, or the families you see each Sunday at church.

Big and small. Near and far. Who do you think made all these families? That's right! God, who makes everything, makes our families.

Long, long ago when God created the earth, He had the perfect plan to make the first family. He created Adam, the first man. And then He created Eve, the first woman, and brought her to Adam.

God joined them together as husband and wife. And from this first human father and mother came every family on earth, right on down to your family!

God's plan to give us families is so kind.

He knows we need someone to care about us and protect us,

to cry with us when we are sad

and celebrate with us when we are happy.

God knows we grow best when we have parents or guardians here on earth who love us and teach us how to honor Him as our King.

Taking care of children is very important to Jesus. The Bible tells about a time when some grown-ups tried to keep children away from Jesus.

But Jesus said, "Let them come to Me!" And He took those children in His arms and blessed them.

God wants dads and moms to tell their children about the wonderful things He has done and how much He loves them. That way children can set their hope in Him instead of in other things.

The Bible says parents should teach their children to say "Yes!" to God. God loves to give Himself to families, to all those who say "Yes!" to Him.

Long ago, it was almost time for Jesus to be born into His own family. When His mother, Mary, visited her older cousin who was also expecting a baby, Mary praised God with a song. The song said that God shows mercy—His kindness—to all those who say "Yes!" to Him, from generation to generation.

Mary followed God. She said "Yes!" to Him. So God gave His mercy to Mary and to the next generation too.

Do you know what a generation is? It means family members who are born around the same time. Your grandparents are one generation. Your parents are another generation. And now you and your brothers and sisters are a new generation.

God promises to give Himself to everyone who says "Yes!" to Him. And He will keep giving Himself from one generation to another . . . to another . . . to another—as long as there are families on earth!

It's not always easy to be part of a family *and* say "Yes!" to God. Maybe your family makes you feel sad sometimes. And it's hard to always be kind and honest.

But you can
remember that your
family is God's plan.
He hears when you
ask Him for help,
and His mercy will
never let you down!

Every morning of your life,
God has new mercies for you.

No family is perfect. But our God uses imperfect families to do amazing things!

Do you remember the Bible story about Jacob and his twelve sons? Joseph was a tattletale, and his brothers were mean and sneaky.

But God used these sinful brothers to start His great big family—amazing!

God loves to give Himself to imperfect families who say "Yes!" to Him.

And what about King Solomon? God gave him more money and wisdom than any other king on earth. But Solomon wasn't perfect. Sometimes he even worshipped idols instead of the one true God.

And yet it was through Solomon's family that God's only Son, Jesus Christ, was born. How wonderful!

Just as He did amazing things
with families in the Bible,
God can use your family to do
amazing things too.

All God asks is that you
keep saying "Yes!" to Him.

You see, a family isn't just a dad and mom and their children. God is there too, working His wonderful plan from one generation to another. And you are an important part of God's plan for your family!

Me?

Will you say "Yes!" to God?
He *loves* it when you do!

And then someday you can teach your own children about God and how much He loves families. You can show them how to say "Yes!" to Him. And His mercy will reach *them* in *their* generation too!

PARENT Connection

B&H KIDS

REMEMBER

His mercy is for those who fear him from generation to generation.—Luke 1:50

READ

Our key verse, Luke 1:50, was spoken by Mary, Jesus's mother. God's mercy reached out to her, a little nobody in the huge Roman Empire. God had promised ages before to build a whole new world, and He came near to Mary with His world-redeeming mercies.

God's purpose of grace starts small, opens wide, and lasts long: "His mercy is for those who fear him from generation to generation." Jesus the Messiah was finally coming—and coming to stay. His new world welcomes you and your family too, from generation to generation.

"Fearing the Lord" means letting God tell your story, saying "Yes!" to Him moment by moment, and letting His will, not yours, define your path, because "his mercy is for those who fear him from generation to generation."

God's mercy is the theme of the whole Bible. Mary's words reflect a well-known verse from the Old Testament: "But the steadfast love of the LORD is from everlasting to everlasting on those who fear him, and his righteousness to children's children" (Psalm 103:17). The God we read about in the Bible is the same God today, even as you read this. And this mighty God is merciful. Stay humble. Stay open. And be ready to say "Yes!" to Him.

THINK

1. Can you tell me about some families in the Bible? How did God use them in amazing ways?
2. Let's talk about the different generations of our family. Who is in our family?
3. Can you think of a time when God showed His mercy to our family and did something amazing for us? Would you like to hear a story about God's mercy to our family?
4. What do you like about our family? Does our family ever make you sad? Tell me about that.
5. Do you see anyone in our family saying "Yes!" to God? When is it hard for you to say "Yes!" to Him?